Margaret, Frank,
and Andy

CYNTHIA RYLANT

Margaret, Frank, and Andy

THREE WRITERS' STORIES

HARCOURT BRACE & COMPANY

San Diego   New York   London

Thank you, Susan Schneider

Requests for permission to make copies of any part of the work
should be mailed to: Permissions Department, Harcourt Brace & Company,
6277 Sea Harbor Drive, Orlando, Florida 32887-6777.

Permissions acknowledgments appear on page 47,
which constitutes a continuation of the copyright page.
Photos on pages 6 and 10 have been vignetted.
Quote on page 44 from *E. B. White: A Biography* by Scott Elledge.
New York: W. W. Norton & Company, 1984.

Library of Congress Cataloging-in-Publication Data
Rylant, Cynthia
Margaret, Frank, and Andy: three writers' stories/Cynthia Rylant.—1st ed.
p. cm
ISBN 0-15-201083-1
1. Authors, American—20th century—Biography—Juvenile literature. 2. Brown,
Margaret Wise, 1910–1952—Biography—Juvenile literature. 3. Baum, L. Frank (Lyman
Frank), 1856–1919—Biography—Juvenile literature. 4. White, E. B. (Elwyn Brooks),
1899–1985—Biography—Juvenile literature. 5. Children's
stories—Authorship—Juvenile literature. I. Title
PS129.R95 1996
810.9'005—dc20
[B] 95-45526

First edition
A C E F D B
Printed in Mexico
Text set in Perpetua
Designed by Lisa Peters

Remembering Leeanne

Margaret, Frank, and Andy

And it was good to be a little Island.

A part of the world

and a world of its own

all surrounded by the bright blue sea.

—The Little Island

Margaret

MARGARET WISE BROWN

SHE LIVED IN AN old house in Maine
that had no electricity and no bathroom
and she called it the Only House. It was
perched all alone on a high sea cliff and was
quite wobbly and rundown but she loved it
dearly, and of course she would, for she was
Margaret Wise Brown.

She was very beautiful, shining with life. Everyone who met her had to remark how pretty she was. She grew up in a house on Long Island, New York, before Long Island became such a busy place as today, and her home was surrounded by woods and beaches and flowers. It was outdoors where she stayed as a little girl, playing with her pets: thirty-six rabbits, two squirrels, some goldfish, and a dog. She remembered this time as a "wild green summer."

Actually, Margaret's whole life was wild and green.

She did the usual things growing up: She went to school, went to college, tried to discover what work she was meant to do and why she was here. She must have had a sense that she might be a writer, for she took a writing class at a university.

But she didn't do very well because she couldn't think of any plots!

Margaret decided to study to be a teacher instead. So she went to Bank Street School, which is famous for training teachers, and there, surrounded by all those children and all those teachers reading to children, the

writer that was buried in her rose up and wrote a story.

It was called *When the Wind Blew,* about an old lady and seventeen cats and one little blue gray kitten. Margaret left the story in a desk drawer and a friend of hers found it and took it off to a publisher, and it was published just as Margaret had written it. Not one word was changed.

Margaret Wise Brown had a gift.

That was in 1937. The next year, 1938, she met Leonard Weisgard, a genteel young man who was quite talented as an artist.

Leonard told her that when he was a boy, his father had taken him around London one day and recorded for him all of the noises of the streets.

Margaret and Leonard both wondered if maybe a book of noises could be done for children, and if maybe the shapes in the books could look like certain noises.

Well, the rest is history, of course, for Margaret and Leonard together made several "noisy books," such as *The Seashore Noisy Book* and *The Country Noisy Book* and other noisy books that are all quite well-known.

Margaret and Leonard became very good friends. Once when they were doing a book together about dogs, Margaret gave Leonard two poodles. She thought having them might help him as he painted. But the poodles were not much help because one night, after Leonard had worked many hours trying to meet a deadline, he put his wet pictures on a table to dry and the two little poodles licked them all clean!

Margaret also loaned Leonard the Only House in Maine to work. He had a tiny room on the top floor, bursting with paints and

brushes and pictures tacked up on the ceiling and walls. And from this room came many books rich with the smell of the sea and the deep quietness of summer evenings and the mystery of fog and boats on the water.

Margaret Wise Brown sometimes lived in a little house in New York City, too, which she called Cobble Court. And its living room was decorated in fur!

She was filled with picture books in her head, and they came to her fast and she had to catch them as quickly as they came. She would grab an old soft pencil nearby and a scrap of paper—grocery lists, old envelopes, whatever she could find all of a sudden— and she would write wildly. She wrote so much that her publishers could hardly keep up with her. She even had to write under another name, Golden MacDonald, to make enough room for herself on the publishers' lists.

She was full of stories and full of fun. If you met her on the street, she might be carrying a kitten jumping about in a basket. She might be pulling along behind a wild little terrier on a leash. She might be on her way to the flower shop. Margaret loved flowers and filled entire rooms in her houses with them. (When she told Leonard Weisgard one day that he needed more flowers in his pictures, he brought in an armful from the fields to paint. The flowers gave him such an attack of hay fever, he couldn't open his eyes for a week!)

Margaret Wise Brown never married, though she intended to. She did not meet anyone she wanted to marry until she was forty-two years old. Then she met someone and fell in love. He was younger than she—twenty-six years old—and, like her, full of zest and a love of life. Margaret went for a short trip to France, planning to marry when she came back home.

But in France she died. No one could believe it. She hadn't been ill. She glowed with life and health. But in France she had to go for a simple operation, and following it, she suddenly died.

Still young, Margaret Wise Brown left behind more than a hundred books for children. Books filled with red barns and little islands and fir trees and fur families and a bunny whispering to a bowl full of mush.

Then, like another famous bunny, a runaway bunny, Margaret Wise Brown went out into the wide, wide world.

While I was in love

I was the happiest man on earth;

but no one can love who has not a heart,

and so I am resolved to ask Oz

to give me one....

—THE TIN WOODMAN,
The Wonderful Wizard of Oz

FRANK

LYMAN FRANK BAUM

YMAN FRANK BAUM's heart

worried him all of his life. He was born with

heart trouble and died with heart trouble,

and this seems fitting for the writer who

created a sentimental tin man.

Known as Frank, he was a disappointment

in nearly every work he ever tried. He had

hundreds of stories in his head, but stories were not considered much use in a man. Stories did not run a successful theater (the theater went broke), or newspaper (the newspaper went broke), or store (the store went broke . . . because Frank wouldn't take money from poor people).

The stories in Frank Baum's head caused him nothing but chaos and poverty, but he could not let them go. He came home each day from whatever job he was failing at and gathered his children and their friends around him for the stories that poured out of him like wine. The stories lived deep inside him, like memories, and some days his mind would be so filled with them, he could barely remember anyone's name.

Frank Baum had grown up in the 1860s with a large family on a beautiful estate in rural New York. He was quiet and frail. His weak heart kept him home. He played alone and gave everything around him a personality, from the tractors to the chickens. (He gave a scarecrow he saw in a field one day so much personality that it chased him in nightmares for months!)

Frank's parents thought him too dreamy, so when he was twelve they sent him to military school. This nearly destroyed him. He was a gentle person and not made for a school in which teachers slapped students in the face or hit them with canes for the smallest mistake. Frank lasted two years there but could take no more. He was returned home, broken.

Back home, though, he soon grew well again, among the green forests, the farm animals, the flowers. He could be a dreamer once more.

When he grew up, Frank Baum seemed to have little talent for anything except being likable and handsome. He was working as an actor when he fell in love with a girl named Maud and married her. Maud's mother was aghast that Maud was marrying this fool! But marry him Maud did, and she and Frank stayed in love for the rest of their lives.

Maud's mother may have had her doubts about Frank, but she knew a good story when she heard one, and she heard good stories coming out of Frank's mouth all the time. "You ought to publish those," she told

Maud Baum

him. Nearly everyone did what Maud's mother said. Even Frank.

So he managed to publish two books for children, which were pretty successful but no blockbusters. Then one night after work he began to tell the children sitting around him a new story.

It was about a farm girl named Dorothy who was blown out of Kansas in a cyclone into an enchanted land. Frank Baum searched his mind for the name of this land. He glanced at a file cabinet nearby. A drawer was marked *O–Z*. The story of Dorothy in the land of Oz came rushing into Frank's head. He followed her down a Road of Yellow Brick, where she met a practical (and unscary) Scarecrow, a weepy Tin Woodman, and a Cowardly Lion.

After putting his children to bed that evening, Frank Baum took up his pen and began to write a new book. He would call it *The Wonderful Wizard of Oz*.

This book made Frank Baum famous, and he lovingly wrote one Oz book after another for his adoring readers. He once promised a new Oz book if a thousand children wrote letters asking for it. A thousand and more did. And sometimes a letter broke his heart, as when a mother wrote to tell him his books had helped her dying son, distracting him from his pain.

Frank and Maud Baum eventually bought a big, comfortable house in California, and they called it Ozcot. Always a lover of beauty, Frank grew a magnificent flower garden (which spelled out *OZ*) and filled an aviary with hundreds of songbirds that would sit on his fingers.

Then, in 1919, Frank's poor heart made

him very ill. He tried to keep writing. But he knew that he was dying.

The Land of Oz is surrounded by a desert, which protects it from the world. Frank Baum always called this desert the Shifting Sands. When finally he died, his dear Maud beside him, his last words were, "Now I can cross the Shifting Sands."

And, of course, everyone in Oz would have been there to meet him.

It is not often that

someone comes along who is

a true friend and a good writer.

Charlotte was both.

—*Charlotte's Web*

Andy

Elwyn Brooks White

E. B. WHITE KNEW he was a writer when he was seven years old. He took one long look at some paper sitting in a typewriter, and he was sure of it. E. B. White certainly would be a good writer one day. What he didn't know was that he would make another good writer—who happened to live in a barn and to have eight legs—famous.

E. B. White grew up with a large, happy family in a big Victorian house in Mount Vernon, New York, in the early 1900s. His parents loved each other and they loved their six children, especially the youngest: Elwyn Brooks, who would be called Andy. Andy White cherished his home. His parents preferred solitude and family, and almost no one was ever invited by.

Andy loved the privacy of this home, the nooks for reading, the sound of boats on the nearby lake. Here he felt safe.

Safety was something Andy thought about a lot. He had been born an anxious boy and worried about everything. He worried about school, about the future, about his health, about death. He did not know he would live a long life, and a safe one. So he worried and feared the worst.

His warm home gave him some comfort. But it was nature and animals that calmed him most. On summer vacations to Maine, Andy felt strong, confident, nearly fearless. He kept pigeons, snakes, turtles, mice, birds,

rabbits, lizards, frogs. He loved sitting and watching them. They were life, and he loved life.

Andy began writing stories as a boy and he won some prizes for them. He knew he didn't want to be a businessman when he grew up. He wanted more freedom than that. He wanted to stay up late, on his own time, typing. He could imagine no other life.

So when he went to college, he kept writing. He became editor of the campus newspaper. Andy's anxieties continued (every day on the way to school he worried that the trolley he was riding would lose its brakes on a hill), but the chance to publish his ideas made him happy. When he graduated he went to New York City to be a reporter.

Andy hated reporting. He quit job after job. He hated being made to write fast. He hated invading other people's privacy. He was a writer, but he was no reporter.

Finally, with a friend, Andy decided to leave everything behind and have an adventure. With two typewriters in the backseat of their car, Andy and his friend set out on a trip across the United States, bound for the West Coast. Along the way they made money however they could: washing dishes, peddling bug killer door-to-door, playing piano, selling poems and stories (plus one of the typewriters).

They had a grand time and they made it all the way to Seattle. When the adventure was over, Andy went back to New York City to live and to look for work again. But he had trouble finding a writing job he liked, and he became depressed. How would he ever make a living?

Then one day Andy wrote a true story

about a waitress spilling buttermilk on him, and he sold the story to a magazine called *The New Yorker*. The editors loved it. They eventually hired him. And one of the editors eventually married him.

Her name was Katharine. She was intelligent and very striking, with dark hair three feet long that she wore pinned to her head. Andy married her and together they had a baby boy. (Katharine nearly died giving birth to this baby. A taxi driver off the street gave blood for her, and this saved her life.)

Being an editor, Katharine understood

writers. So when one day Andy asked her to leave New York City and to live on a farm in Maine with him, she said yes. She thought it would be good for his writing. Of course, she was right. Living in nature again, feeling like a boy, Andy wrote his first children's book, *Stuart Little*, about a mouselike child born to human parents. (The strangeness of this so shocked a New York City librarian that she tried to stop the book's publication!)

The book was a success and Andy wanted to write another. And it was the living among pigs and spiders, rats, geese, and

sheep that guided Andy White to a new story: a story about a pig named Wilbur, a spider named Charlotte, and salvation. The story was called *Charlotte's Web*. It was written in a boathouse that had one chair, one table, one stove, one typewriter. And it became the most popular American children's book ever published.

E. B. White—Andy—once said, "All that I hope to say in books, all that I ever hope to say, is that I love the world."

He wrote one more children's book, *The Trumpet of the Swan,* and then his beloved wife, Katharine, died and he did not write any more books. He planted an oak tree at her grave and went back to his farm, where he tended the animals, fixed things, and wrote letters to old friends and young readers.

Then, after eighty-six years of worrying that he would die, E. B. White at last let go of the world he loved so much. He left having known "the glory of everything." And, like Charlotte, having made it more radiant.

Grateful acknowledgment is made for permission
to use the following material:

Jacket photos: See acknowledgments for pages 2, 18, 32.

Text excerpt, page viii: From *The Little Island* by Golden
MacDonald, Leonard Weisgard, illustrator. Copyright
1946 by Doubleday, a division of Bantam Doubleday
Dell Publishing Group, Inc. Used by permission of the
publisher.

Photo, page 2: Courtesy of Archives, Fishburn Library,
Hollins College, Roanoke, Virginia

Photo, page 6: By Consuelo Kanaga, *Margaret Wise Brown*.
Courtesy of The Brooklyn Museum, 82.65.1836; gift of
Wallace Putnam from the Estate of Consuelo Kanaga.
The photo has been vignetted for this book.

Photo, page 10: By Consuelo Kanaga, *Untitled (The Only House)*. Courtesy of The Brooklyn Museum, 82.65.1820; gift of Wallace Putnam from the Estate of Consuelo Kanaga. The photo has been vignetted for this book.

Photos, pages 18, 23, 25: Courtesy of the L. Frank Baum Collection, Alexander Mitchell Library, Aberdeen, South Dakota

Photos, pages 32, 36, 41, 43: Courtesy of the Estate of E. B. White